Hook Norton Brewery

Caversham Lakes

Broughton Castle

Great Haseley Windmill

Blenheim Palace

Postcards from
Oxfordshire

Swinford Toll Bridge

Burford

'Cotswold Lion' Sheep

White Horse ~ Uffington

Abingdon

First published 2024 by Whitefoot PR Ltd, Shelsley Beauchamp, Worcestershire, WR6 6RB, UK

ISBN 978-1-7392866-4-4

British Library Cataloguing in Publication (CIP) Programme. A catalogue record for this book is available from the British Library

Designed by Whitefoot PR, Worcestershire, WR6 6RB, UK
Text by Michelle Whitefoot

www.michaelwhitefoot.co.uk

All images copyright © Michael Whitefoot

Introduction

Located in the very heart of England, spread across the verdant hills, woods and farmlands between London and the Cotswolds, the land-locked county of Oxfordshire's unique combination of agriculture and academia makes it one of the most historically interesting and frequently visited in the United Kingdom, drawing around 7 million visitors each year.

A chief reason why Oxfordshire is on so many 'must-see' lists is the jewel in its crown, the city of Oxford. Home to the oldest university in the English-speaking world, Oxford's 43, largely Gothic and Baroque-style colleges inspired Victorian poet Matthew Arnold's description of a 'sweet City with her dreaming spires'. Complementing the city's global reputation as a seat of knowledge, technology and culture are the astonishing collections housed in the Ashmolean Museum of art and archaeology, the Museum of Natural History and the ancient Bodleian Old Library. Those who explore beyond Oxford, however, know that the rest of the county shines just as brightly. Dotted across its countryside are thriving market towns such as Banbury, Witney, Bicester, Abingdon, Henley and Wantage, plus innumerable characterful villages. Northwest of Oxford, the Baroque masterpiece of Blenheim Palace, birthplace of Britain's wartime Prime Minister Sir Winston Churchill, stands splendidly in glorious parklands. To the southwest, the prehistoric Uffington White Horse chalk figure prancing across a hilltop is one of England's most recognisable icons. Impressive natural features also abound. Oxfordshire's fertile landscapes support a rich farming history, and part of the Thames – England's longest river - weaves from west to east. Oxfordshire also forms part of the Chilterns National Landscape and the renowned Cotswolds region, including picturesque villages such as Burford and Chipping Norton.

As always, whether you're a visitor to these memorable locations or a proud local, there's no better way of remembering your favourite destinations than a picture postcard capturing the scene. Perhaps the image recalls a special memory, historic landmark, or a stunning view encountered on our travels. We might even gain new perspectives from the air, such as a bird's eye view of rolling landscapes or a fascinating townscape far below. These are the kinds of memories that Worcestershire-based professional landscape photographer and entrepreneur, Michael Whitefoot, aims to create every day through his postcards, gifts and souvenir ranges. Now this book, *Postcards from Oxfordshire*, brings together 144 of Michael's most spectacular postcard landscapes into a single volume, capturing the essence of this much-admired county. So come with us on a journey through some of Oxfordshire's most memorable views, in a stunning postcard collection to keep forever.

Great Coxwell Barn

Farington Folly

Minster Lovell

Milton Manor House

Oxford

Carfax Tower ~ Oxford

'Bridge of Sighs' ~ Oxford

Oxford Botanic Gardens

Oxfordshire

Index of photos

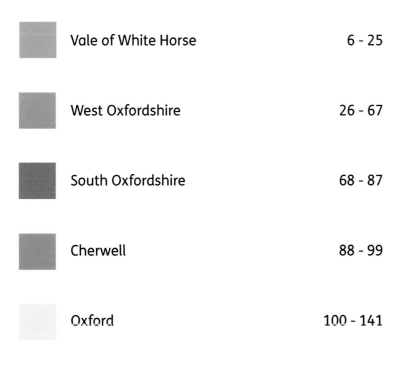

Vale of White Horse   6 - 25

West Oxfordshire   26 - 67

South Oxfordshire   68 - 87

Cherwell   88 - 99

Oxford   100 - 141

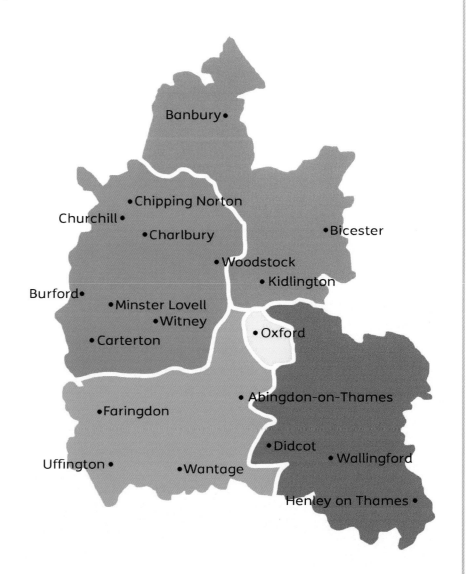

Banbury•

•Chipping Norton

Churchill•

•Charlbury

•Bicester

•Woodstock

•Kidlington

Burford•

•Minster Lovell

•Witney

•Oxford

•Carterton

•Abingdon-on-Thames

•Faringdon

•Didcot

•Wallingford

Uffington •

•Wantage

Henley on Thames •

Vale of White Horse

Forming the south-west region of Oxfordshire, bordering the Berkshire Downs and north-east Wiltshire, the Vale of White Horse is an attractive rural district of chalk hills and ancient settlements, that is home to several of the county's most historic connections.

The district owes its name to a prehistoric landmark at its south-west tip: the world-famous, Bronze Age white chalk figure of a White Horse, carved into the Berkshire Downs near Uffington. The 360 ft (110 m) long design leaps across the folds of White Horse Hill, forming an iconic symbol of British ancient history that is a favourite sight from miles around. Just a mile away stands Wayland's Smithy, an atmospheric, early Neolithic long barrow once believed to have been the home of Wayland, the Saxon god of metal working. Rising up from the flatter landscape further east, the Wittenham Clumps – a pair of chalk hills, topped with trees – are another visual landmark and popular walking trail.

History has also given the Vale's largest market town, Wantage – originally a small Roman settlement – a Royal claim to fame: it was the birthplace of Anglo-Saxon King Alfred 'the Great' in 849 AD. Today, a Victorian-built statue of Alfred makes an imposing focal point in the town's busy market place, which is surrounded by 18th century shop facades. Further west lies another of the Vale's towns, Faringdon – the first capital of the Anglo-Saxon kingdom of Wessex. Strategically situated on an ancient, five-way road junction that drew business from across the country, Faringdon has been a thriving trading point for agricultural and animal produce since 1218, and its 17th century Old Town Hall still stands today. On the town's outskirts is 140 ft (43 m) high Faringdon Folly Tower, from whose ramparts visitors can enjoy panoramic views across five counties. To the east of the Vale region, the easy river crossing point offered by Abingdon-on-Thames made it a thriving centre for wool trading, weaving and clothing manufacture from medieval to Victorian times. Claiming to be England's oldest occupied town, Abingdon's historic importance is still evidenced today in the impressive structures of its County Hall Museum, Guildhall and many almshouses.

Elsewhere in the Vale of White Horse are a scattering of quieter villages such as Ardington, Ashbury, Buckland and Kingston Bagpuize. Many of these feature pretty, often thatched stone cottages, as well as boasting substantial churches and imposing manor houses. Amongst these are the privately-owned, Palladian masterpiece Buckland House; the 13th century Charney Manor, now a conference centre and retreat; and Georgian-style Kingston Bagpuize House, which is open to the public.

Built in the 18th century by architect Inigo Jones, for King George III's lace maker, elegant Milton Manor House forms part of nearby Abingdon's cloth-related heritage

Where the River Thames broadens on the outskirts of Abingdon-on-Thames, 15th century Abingdon Bridge provides a vital crossing point to the countryside beyond

In Abingdon-on-Thames, 12th century St Nicholas's Church – known as the 'little church by the gate' – was part of Abingdon Abbey. The Guildhall stands alongside it

10   With their distinctive chimney stacks, Brick Alley Almshouses, built in 1718, overlook the River Thames in Abingdon and continue to provide housing for elderly residents

The market square in Abingdon is dominated by the 17th century County Hall. Originally housing an arched market space, with courtroom above, it is now a museum

Above the rural, Saxon village of Ashbury, in the south-western tip of Oxfordshire, the Church of St Mary the Virgin dates back to the 12th century

Ashbury village contains some of Oxfordshire's most photogenic cottages, including these traditional thatched examples edged with hollyhocks

West of Oxford, the vast Farmoor Reservoir purifies water from the River Thames to supply Oxford and Swindon. Oxford Sailing Club lies on its eastern bank

Much of the village of Buckland was built as an estate to house workers employed at magnificent Buckland House, built around 1750 in Palladian style

The Manger is an unusually shaped valley near Uffington, formed in the Ice Age, which folklore suggests is the nocturnal feeding place of the White Horse figure above it

Carved into the white chalk bedrock above The Manger, the 374 ft (114 m) long, Bronze Age White Horse figure is thought to represent a Celtic tribe's horse goddess

East of Wantage, the village of Ardington is part of a large, 19th century country estate. Its Church of Holy Trinity, built in the Early English style, dates to around 1200

Waylands Smithy is an atmospheric, Early Neolithic long barrow (burial mound) near the Uffington White Horse. Its two chambers were constructed around 3500 BC

Near the market town of Faringdon and encircled by woodland, Faringdon Folly's impressive, 100 ft (30.5 m) tower was built in 1935, with views across five counties

The enormous, Cotswold stone Great Coxwell Tithe Barn is the only surviving part of a 13th century grange that once provided income to Beaulieu Abbey

Now a conference centre and retreat, 13th century Charney Manor in Charney Bassett was originally built as a grange of Abingdon Abbey

Between Radcot and Faringdon, 13th century Radcot Bridge, the oldest bridge still spanning the River Thames, features pointed arches of Cotswolds stone

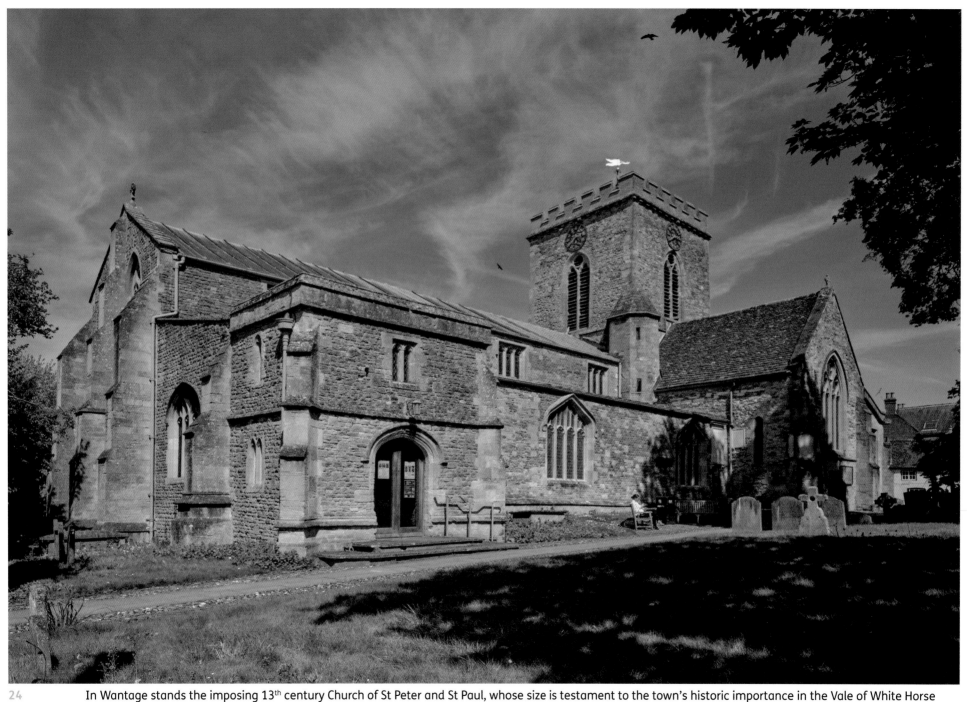

In Wantage stands the imposing 13th century Church of St Peter and St Paul, whose size is testament to the town's historic importance in the Vale of White Horse

Wantage was the birthplace in 849 AD of King Alfred 'the Great'. This 1877 statue of him, sculpted by a relative of Queen Victoria, overlooks the town's marketplace today

West Oxfordshire

The mainly rural district of West Oxfordshire, which borders the county of Gloucestershire, is perhaps best known as part of the world-famous Cotswolds National Landscape – the range of gently sloping hills whose golden limestone has characterised the region's picturesque architecture for centuries. While the Oxfordshire Cotswolds form the northern portion of this district, its south east comprises a sweeping clay floodplain. In these lowlands, limestone deposited from the hills by prehistoric rivers created extensive gravel terraces that are still mined today – with many of the former pit workings now flooded to form a patchwork of fishing and wildlife lakes. Adding to the area's waterways are the meandering Windrush and Evenlode rivers, as well as the River Thames which hugs West Oxfordshire's southerly edge.

The Cotswolds name derives from the Old English words for high, open land ('wolds') and the pens ('cots') that housed the iconic 'Lion' sheep that have been farmed there since Roman times. By the Middle Ages, the Cotswolds had become so renowned for its fleeces that its towns became prosperous from the lucrative wool and clothing trades. Today that success remains evident in the region's many honey-coloured stone cottages, manor houses, public buildings and impressive 'wool churches' funded by wealthy merchants. Some of the most attractive of these Cotswolds towns are found in West Oxfordshire. Chipping Norton, towards the north, was a major wool market ('chipping' meaning 'market') and is still home to the fine wool church of St Mary, as well as the former Bliss Tweed Mill. At the western edge of Oxfordshire lies the coaching town of Burford, where woolsack-shaped tombs can still be seen at St John's Church. In nearby Minster Lovell, thatched cottages create an idyllic setting. The smaller villages of Shipton-under-Wychwood and Stanton Harcourt are also home to many photogenic cottages.

West Oxfordshire also boasts an especially important architectural treasure with legendary political connections, that today is one of England's most visited stately homes. Standing in extensive parklands, on the outskirts of the fine Georgian town of Woodstock, is Blenheim Palace – England's largest Baroque building and birthplace of former British Prime Minister, Sir Winston Churchill. Nearby, St Martin's Church in Bladon contains Churchill's grave.

The West Oxfordshire district is also home to the largest market town in the Cotswolds, Witney. As well as its many notable buildings, including the 18th century Holloways Almshouses and Norman-built St Mary the Virgin Church, two ancient sites near Witney demonstrate the area's even older importance: the remains of North Leigh Roman Villa, and a 5,000 year-old henge and stone circle known as the Devil's Quoits.

Asthall village is home to Asthall Manor – a Jacobean manor that in the 1920s was the childhood home of the Mitford sisters. St Nicholas's Church stands opposite

The size and grandeur of Blenheim Palace near Woodstock, built between 1705 and 1722, makes it an unforgettable sight for around one million visitors each year

Blenheim Palace overlooks rolling parklands, 160 acre (65 hectare) Queen Pool lake and a Grand Bridge; all landscapes created in the 1760s by Lancelot 'Capability' Brown

Blenheim Palace is the family seat of the Dukes of Marlborough, and where former British Prime Minister Sir Winston Churchill was born during a family visit in 1874

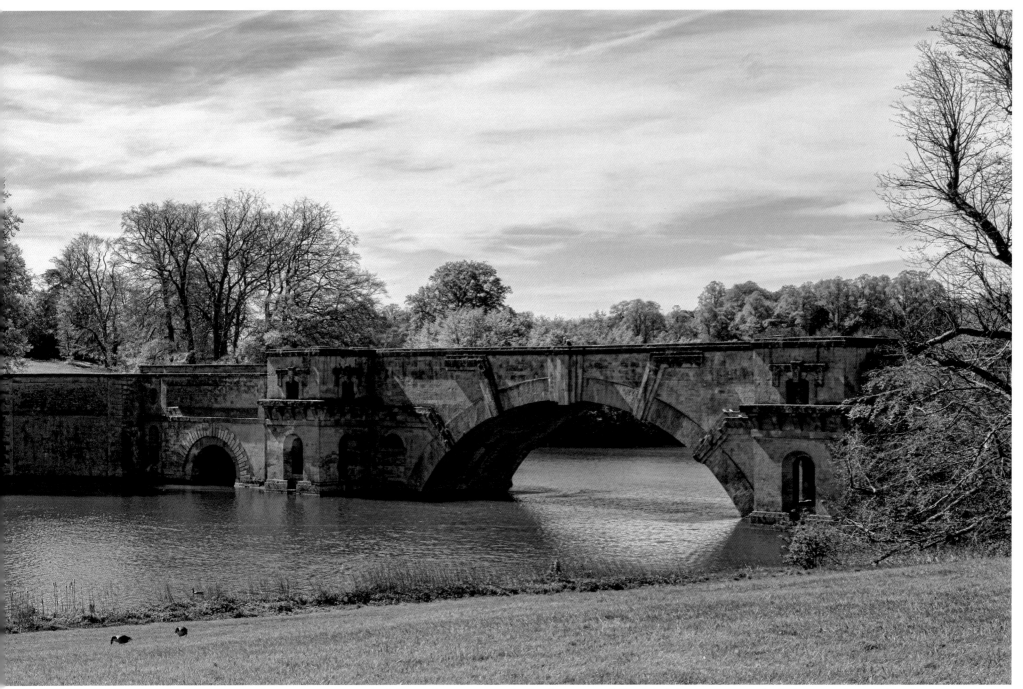

In the 2020s, Queen Pool lake underwent a two-year dredging project to restore its depth to over 6 ft (2 m), helping to preserve Blenheim Palace's stunning vistas

Blenheim's immense Column of Victory, inspired by the Piazza Navona pillar in Rome, was built in 1727 to commemorate the Duke of Marlborough's military successes

The extensive 2,100 acre (850 hectare) Blenheim Palace estate boasts varied natural habitats, including parklands, grazed grassland, woodland, rivers and lakes

Visitors to Blenheim Palace can stroll through breathtaking formal gardens including water terraces, an Italian garden and the Churchill Memorial Garden

A masterpiece of Baroque architecture, Blenheim Palace contains 187 rooms and is bigger than London's main Royal residence, Buckingham Palace

In the centre of Blenheim's Queen Pool lake, Queen Elizabeth Island is a haven for wildlife. The lake is encrcled by a 45-minute walk

The beautifully designed, far-reaching formal and informal landscapes surrounding majestic Blenheim Palace can be fully appreciated from the air

Visitors reach Blenheim Palace's magnificent principal entrance via the extensive, paved Great Courtyard

Blenheim stands on the site of a 12th century palace built in 1129 by Henry I. The land and money to build it were gifted to the 1st Duke of Marlborough by Queen Anne

Victorian St Martin's Church in Bladon near Woodstock, is best known as the burial place of Sir Winston Churchill, his wife Clementine and other family members

Although Churchill was given a state funeral in St Paul's Cathedral, London, his wishes were to be buried in this country churchyard, close to his birthplace, Blenheim

A bird's-eye view of picturesque Burford reveals its part tree-lined main street sloping down to the River Windrush, with St John the Baptist Church in the foreground

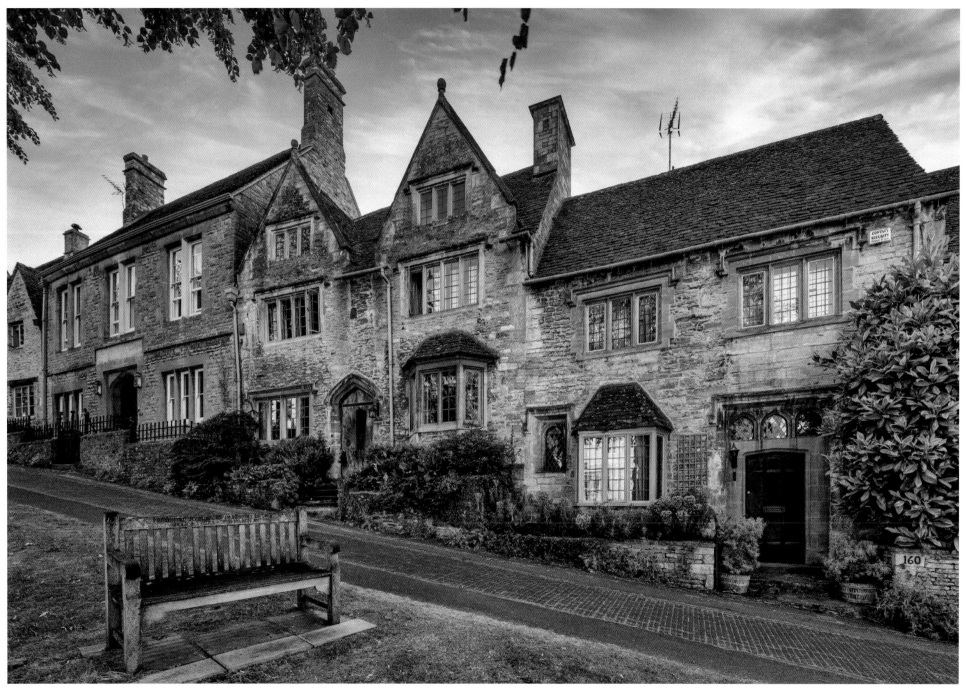

The top of Burford's sloping High Street is lined by fascinating Tudor and Georgian houses, built from honey-coloured Cotswolds stone at the height of the wool trade

The elaborate 'woolsack'-topped tombs at St John the Baptist Church in Burford date from the 1700s

Burford's splendid St John the Baptist Church was completed in the 15th century by wool merchants who had prospered from the Cotswolds Lion sheep's 'Golden Fleece'

St Mary's Church in Witney reflects the town's wool-trade wealth in the Middle Ages. Its landmark 156 ft (48 m) spire is visible across the town

This row of 18ᵗʰ century Holloway Almshouses in Witney, named after their cloth merchant founder, were built to house 'six aged, unmarried women' from the locality

Chipping Norton's imposing Town Hall, which stands in the Market Place, was built in Palladian style in 1842

These Almshouses in the market town of Chipping Norton were founded in 1640

All Saints Church in Churchill, built in 1826, has a striking west tower which is a two-thirds scale copy of Magdalen College bell tower in Oxford

Near Witney lie the remains of North Leigh Roman Villa, a fine 'courtyard villa' that boasted three bath suites, 19 mosaic floors and 11 rooms with underfloor heating

Believed to be up to 5,000 years old, the 390 ft (120 m) wide Devil's Quoits henge and stone circle near Stanton Harcourt overlooks a flooded gravel pit lake

Chastleton House, positioned between Moreton-in-March and Chipping Norton, is one of the finest, most complete Jacobean country houses in England

The Georgian-built, still-active Swinbrook Toll Bridge, in the hamlet of Swinbrook, enables travellers to cross the River Thames near Eynsham lock

Some of Stanton Harcourt's sturdy, Jurassic limestone cottages have 'risen loaf' roofs, formed from an unusually deep dome of thatch

Nestled in the village of Brize Norton, close to the UK's largest Royal Air Force (RAF) base, this Norman church is the only one in England dedicated to St Britius

Impressive 19th century Bliss Tweed Mill near Chipping Norton, where fabric for military uniforms and horse blankets was originally made, has been converted into homes

The 108 ft (33 m) diameter 'King's Men' stone circle near Chipping Norton – whose stones by legend represent 'a monarch and his courtiers petrified by a witch'

Shipton-under-Wychwood, one of three villages taking their name from the old Wychwood Forest, lies on the River Evenlode and features a wealth of Cotswolds charm

A row of characterful Cotswold stone cottages in Minster Lovell, featuring traditional cottage garden planting

Climbing roses adorn a large, honey-coloured thatched cottage in the village of Minster Lovell

Much of St Mary's Church in Swinbrook dates back to the 12th century. Its churchyard contains the gravestones of four of the famed Mitford sisters

St Mary's Church contains two sets of 17th century reclining effigies, each commemorating three generations of the wealthy Fettiplace family who held Swinbrook's manor

Still farmed today, the Cotswolds 'Lion' breed of sheep is renowned for its luxuriant 'Golden Fleece' that brought prosperity to the region from medieval times

Heythrop Park is an 18th century Italian Baroque country house set in 440 acres (178 hectares) of parkland, that today is run as a large hotel

In the Vale of White Horse near Uffington and Wayland's Smithy, clay soil creates a low-lying, open landscape that is largely farmland

The area's broad agricultural fields are often edged by deciduous woodland perimeters; some featuring square, forested 'islands'

South Oxfordshire

Neighbouring the counties of Buckinghamshire to the east, and Berkshire to the south, the district of South Oxfordshire combines a mainly agricultural economy with several principal towns, a scattering of rural villages and many natural and manmade locations of interest.

Similar to more central parts of the county, much of South Oxfordshire owes its farming heritage to a broad, clay valley drained by the River Thames. Towards its south-east corner, however, rise parts of two, protected National Landscapes: the beech-forested hillsides and rich farmlands of the Chiltern Hills, and the more open, chalk hills of the North Wessex Downs.

The majority of South Oxfordshire locals live and work in the district's four main towns: Didcot, Wallingford, Henley and Thame. Of these, Didcot – perhaps best known for its railway museum and remaining natural gas power plant – is the main urban centre, as well as a well-connected location for commuters to London. The nearby market town of Wallingford, which stands on the River Thames, boasts the ruins of Wallingford Castle – built as a Thames Valley stronghold after the town helped William the Conqueror take the English throne in 1066. In the south-east, Henley-on-Thames has been voted one of the best places to live in England. Adding to its still-traditional centre, the town has the Chiltern landscape on its doorstep and optimises its River Thames location by hosting the world's best-known annual rowing regatta. Further north, the bustling market town of Thame, with it's long, 'boat-shaped' high street, has become famous in recent years as the filming location for the fictional town of Causton in the British TV crime drama, *Midsomer Murders*. Amongst South Oxfordshire's smaller villages of note are Dorchester, with its handsome, Saxon-built abbey; picturesque Clifton Hampden, lined with numerous thatched cottages; and Ewelme, whose historic chalk brook water-cress beds are now run as a nature reserve.

South Oxfordshire is also home to many fine, historic manor houses. Examples include 18th century villa Nuneham House, east of Abingdon, and country houses such as Nuffield Place, Stonor Park, Grey's Court and Mapledurham House, all of which lie in nooks of the Chiltern Hills.

Other points of interest draw visitors to the great outdoors. Harcourt Arboretum, a satellite of Oxford University's Botanic Garden, has the county's widest selection of rare trees. Travellers can also look out for popular landmarks, such as the tree-topped hills of the Wittenham Clumps, or Great Haseley windmill, standing tall above open farmlands south-east of Oxford.

Nuneham House, a Palladian-style 18th century villa set in 55 acres (22 hectares) of riverside pleasure grounds, is currently used as a retreat centre

Kelmscott Manor House, built around 1600, was the summer retreat of Victorian textile designer, poet and father of the Arts & Crafts movement, William Morris

In the mid-20th century, Nuffield Place was the Arts & Crafts-era home of Lord Nuffield, philanthropist and founder of the Morris Motor Company

Ewelme Park House is a Lutyens-style country mansion built in 1913, set in extensive gardens overlooking the Chiltern Escarpment

Visitors to Didcot Railway Centre can savour the golden age of steam, travelling on heritage steam trains dating from Victorian times to the 1960s

Described as Oxfordshire's 'twin peaks', Wittenham Clumps comprise two, 300 ft (91 m) high hills, each topped with a crown of trees

Silhouetted between sky and hills, the Wittenham Clumps form a local landmark and are one of the most visited, public green spaces in the region

Henley-on-Thames is renowned for its prestigious, annual Henley Royal Regatta, which attracts top rowing competitors and thousands of visitors from around the world

The estate of Le Manoir aux Quat'Saisons dates from 1225. Today it is a celebrated country house hotel and restaurant with its own herb and vegetable gardens

Standing on the site of a 7th century cathedral, Dorchester Abbey is one of the earliest Christian sites in Britain, and all that remains of a fine Augustinian abbey

The pale, ruined walls of 11th century Wallingford Castle stand just outside Wallingford village, overlooking the River Thames and medieval road bridge

Nestled in an ancient, 12th century farming estate on the River Thames, Mapledurham House is an outstanding Elizabethan stately home with two hidden 'priest holes'

The grounds of the Mapledurham estate include a rushing weir and the last, still-working water mill on the River Thames

The site of Greys Court, an elegant Tudor country house near Henley-on-Thames, was first recorded as the seat of the de Grey family in the Domesday Book of 1086

Harcourt Arboretum offers the chance to explore 130 acres (52 hectares) of British woodland, wildflower meadows and rare trees from around the world

Sitting alongside the Thames in beautiful Clifton Hampden village, St Michael and All Angels Church has parts dating back to 1180 and boasts an unusually fine spire

In the most southerly tip of Oxfordshire, just outside Reading, Caversham Lakes were formed from former gravel pits on the River Thames floodplain

Stonor Park, a country house and deer park in the Chiltern Hills, has belonged to one family for 850 years, making it one of Britain's oldest family homes

Clifton Hampden Bridge was built to span the River Thames in 1864. It features seven Gothic arches and pointed abutments, as well as a toll house at the south end

Cherwell

The northernmost part of Oxfordshire is known as the Cherwell district – named after the River Cherwell, whose broad, calm waters carve the region in two from north to south before joining the River Thames at Oxford.

Either side of this Cherwell Valley, the landscapes are varied. Farmland plateaus and rolling pastures dominate the west of the district, while further east lie wide swathes of fields and woodland, which in turn give way to a long clay valley.

Two main market towns help to drive Cherwell's varied professional, technical, retail and agricultural economy. The larger of these is Banbury, set amidst gentle hills in the north of the district. The town's name has gained legendary status thanks to the much-loved nursery rhyme, 'Ride a cock horse to Banbury Cross' where a 'fine lady on a white horse' could be seen. Today, where the roads from Oxford, Warwick and Shipston-on-Stour meet in central Banbury, visitors can still admire the Banbury Cross Victorian memorial which marked the marriage of Queen Victoria's eldest daughter. Completing the tableau, a modern, life-size bronze Fine Lady statue stands nearby, depicting a May Queen on horseback. Banbury's other attractions include independent shops in the Old Town, a museum and historic boatyard.

Cherwell's second key town, Bicester, combines a range of modern and old stone buildings, a colourful weekly market and independent shops. It is also home to the world-famous luxury shopping destination, Bicester Village; as well as Bicester Heritage, a centre for vintage car and motorcycle restoration.

In the south of Cherwell district lies Kidlington. One of England's largest villages, Kidlington's rural heritage remains visible in the many, well-preserved historic buildings in its old centre. Other villages include Islip, which stands at an ancient ford on the River Ray; and Adderbury, which, like several hamlets in the area, boasts a number of honey-coloured ironstone houses as well as the exceptionally ornate St Mary's Church.

Several manor houses of interest are also dotted across the Cherwell area. Near Banbury is Broughton Castle, a fortified, ironstone-built 14th century manor house with spectacular moat, whose edifice is familiar to many from a string of major films. In the centre of the district, the landscape gardens of Rousham House are a rare, unaltered example of 18th century designer William Kent's work. Meanwhile, the classic Georgian appearance of Tusmore House, whose parklands can be visited, belies its 2004 construction date.

Elegant 13th century St Mary's Church in Adderbury is one of the finest parish churches in Oxfordshire, remarkable for its wealth of carvings and sculptures

Marking the crossroads in the town of Banbury, ornate Banbury Cross was erected in 1859 to commemorate the wedding of Queen Victoria's eldest daughter

This 2005 bronze statue next to Banbury Cross represents the 'fine lady upon a white horse' mentioned in the beloved nursery rhyme that made Banbury famous

Magnificent Broughton Castle is a medieval, moated and fortified manor house in Broughton, near Banbury. In the 17th century it was a centre of opposition to Charles I

Handcrafted brewing still takes place in the Victorian 'tower' brewing plant of Hook Norton Brewery, with the processes flowing logically from the top floor down

Attractive Islip village was the birthplace of King Edward 'the Confessor' in 1004. When he later founded London's Westminster Abbey, he gifted Islip to the abbey

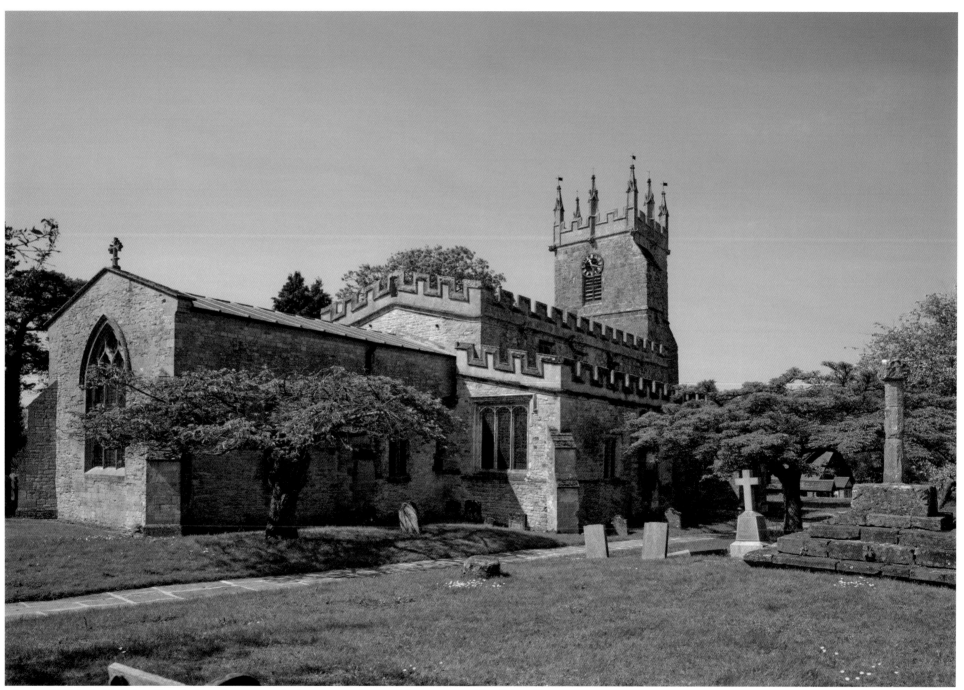

Parts of Islip's St Nicholas Church date from around 1200. Westminster Abbey's ownership of the village means it still retains the right to nominate the church's rectors

Traditional British red telephone boxes outside a shop in Bicester Shopping Village

Bicester Village offers more than 150 outlet shopping boutiques

A rare moment of calm in Bicester Village before opening time

Designer brands compete for shoppers' attention at Bicester Village

Bicester Village's 1.2 mile (1.9 km) long 'High Street' is as long as London's Oxford Street, and attracts seven million bargain-hunters from across the world each year

The white French stone of neo-Georgian style Tusmore House, built in 2004 on the site of a long-demolished 18th century manor, stands out against the landscape

Rousham House, nestled in the countryside west of Bicester, is surrounded by remarkable 17th century gardens designed by architect and designer William Kent

Oxford

Centrally situated in the very heart of the county, the city of Oxford is the jewel in Oxfordshire's crown. Conjuring images of learning and academia, punting along misty waterways, and the romantic University skyline that Victorian poet Matthew Arnold described as 'that sweet City with her dreaming spires', Oxford forms the hub of the county's economy, reputation and tourist trade.

No visit to the city would be complete without taking the time to appreciate its single most important asset: The University of Oxford. Consistently ranked as the world's top university, it has more than 26,000 students, almost half of them international, studying multiple disciplines across 43 colleges, societies and permanent private halls. Teaching in some form has existed at Oxford since 1096, with the oldest existing colleges of University, Balliol and Merton established in the 13th century. Since then, new colleges have opened continually over the centuries, the most recent founded in 2019. This rich heritage oozes from the creamy-coloured, local stone of the many college buildings as you explore the streets. With most of the University's older colleges located centrally, and sometimes partially open to visitors, it is easy to peep in and experience the atmosphere of their historic quadrangles and intricate, often Gothic or Baroque architecture. The city's majestic 16th century Christ Church Cathedral, also a college chapel, is within equally easy reach.

Many of Oxford's other finest buildings are also linked with the history of Oxford University. Amongst these are the celebrated Bodleian Old Library – the University's principal library and one of the oldest and largest in Europe. Connected to it by an underground passage is the domed Radcliffe Camera library. Another landmark for sightseers is Hertford Bridge, popularly known as the 'Bridge of Sighs' – a striking skyway spanning a lane between two parts of Hertford College. The Radcliffe Observatory in Green Templeton College was Oxford University's astronomical observatory for centuries. Other architectural jewels around the city include the elegant, D-shaped Sheldonian Theatre designed by a young Sir Christopher Wren; the handsome Arts and Crafts-built Rhodes House; and Carfax Tower, the remains of a 12th century church, now overlooking shopping streets below.

Those seeking art, archaeology and natural history also have a treat in store in central Oxford, with the astonishing, world-famous collections at the Ashmolean Museum, Museum of Natural History and Pitt Rivers Museum all within walking distance. Shoppers can take their pick from a generous selection of major and independent stores, as well as a traditional covered market of food and craft stalls. There are also outdoor pleasures, from a stroll through Oxford Botanic Garden – the oldest in Britain – to taking an idyllic punt along the peaceful River Cherwell, on which Oxford stands.

An aerial view of central Oxford reveals the glory of its magnificently ornamented University quadrangles and public buildings, most built in creamy local limestone

The renowned Ashmolean Museum began in 1682, when antiquary Elias Ashmole gifted his collection to the University. Right is the Taylor Institution library

The striking, polychromatic brickwork of 19th century Keble College Chapel was a hallmark of architect William Butterfield and designed to stand out from other colleges

The front quad of Oxford's Oriel College has 'Regnante Carolo' carved into the parapet, commemorating the reign of Charles I when the quad was finished

As a mainly academic research institution, 15th century All Souls College is unique in having no undergraduate members, only teaching and research Fellows

Carfax Tower is the only remains of St Martin's Church, Oxford's city church from 1122. Its east façade features two 'quarter boys' who strike the bells every 15 minutes

Peaceful, 17th century Canterbury Quad in St John's College contains ranks of columns, above which sit the college's Old Library and Laudian Library

The distinctive 'stripes' of the Old Bodleian Library's Jacobean Gothic Schools Quadrangle surround a statue of the 3rd Earl of Pembroke, a former University Chancellor

Recently redeveloped Rhodes House, which opened in 1829, is topped by a curved green dome. The building houses the Rhodes Trust educational charity

Founded in 1621, the University of Oxford Botanic Garden is the oldest botanical garden in England, with its entrance proudly marked by the Danby Gate

Oxford Botanic Garden is home to more than 5,000 plant species laid out across gardens and glasshouses – here with Magdalen College tower in the background

Oxford University Press, renowned for publishing academic and educational books, occupies a handsome, early 19th century building in the Oxford suburb of Jericho

Opposite Oxford University Press is the curving glass structure of the Blavatnik School of Government, a school of Public Policy founded by the University of Oxford in 2010

The cloistered quadrangle of 15th century Magdelene College (pronounced 'Maudlin') is surrounded by wisteria and hydrangeas, and overlooked by the Great Tower

The circular, Baroque style of 18th century Radcliffe Camera (meaning 'room'), which houses a working library, makes it one of the most distinctive buildings in Oxford

Punting in a traditional, hand-crafted boat on the River Cherwell, is one of the quintissential, old-fashioned delights of a visit to Oxford

E·LARGA·MVNIFICENTIA

CAECILII RHODES

This statue of British colonialist Cecil Rhodes, a student at Oriel College in the 1870s, overlooks Oxford's High Street from an Oriel College building

Sitting on Oxford's High Street, Queen's College is one of the University's oldest, founded in 1341. Its frontage features a cupola with statue of Queen Caroline of Ansbach

The fascinating Holywell Cemetery behind 12th century St Cross Church in Oxford contains scores of intricately carved crosses, some in a braided Celtic style

The Christ Church War Memorial Garden, overlooked by 12th century Christ Church Cathedral behind, was created in 1926 to commemorate the First World War

Grandly beautiful Christ Church College was founded in 1546 by King Henry VIII, comprising both a college for the University and the cathedral for the diocese of Oxford

Oxford University's New College was founded in 1379 with part of the much-older City Wall incorporated into its perimeter – which it is still required to maintain today

New College's front quadrangle, with its Chapel, hall, libraries and sleeping quarters located around a central quad, became the model for many later colleges

Anglo-Saxon St Michael Tower was built from rubble and coral limestone

The Martyrs' Memorial commemorates three Protestant martyrs who died in 1555

All Souls College was built in the mid-1400s and stands on Oxford's High Street. Today its quadrangle still houses academics' bedrooms, with the Chapel at the far end

The BMW Group's vast Mini car assembly plant in Cowley, Oxford, is part of the city's long-standing automotive heritage and manfactures around 1,000 cars a day

Central Oxford's Covered Market dates back to the 1770s

The venue is home to over 50 specialist independent traders

The Covered Market is one of the oldest, continually operating markets in England

Here, shoppers can also take advantage of a selection of cafés and bars

Wolvercote Cemetery just outside Oxford is the final resting place of *The Lord of the Rings* and *The Hobbit* author J.R.R. Tolkein, with his wife Edith

An aerial view across Oxford to the countryside beyond, taken from above the city's South Park on Headington Hill

Oxford University's fascinating Museum of Natural History is housed in a striking, Victorian neo-Gothic building with a glass and cast iron roof

The Natural History Museum's exhibits include the famous Oxfordshire dinosaurs

The Museum's cast iron columns are ornamented to represent tree branches

Adjacent Pitt Rivers Museum specialises in anthropology and archaeology

The Natural History Museum's collections are internationally important

Directly opposite the Ashmolean Museum, the Victorian-built Randolph Hotel offers guests a luxurious stay in Gothic splendour

Trading since 1879, Blackwell of Oxford is the largest academic and specialist bookshop in the UK, containing a surprisingly vast network of rooms to explore

Handsome Radcliffe Observatory was the astronomical observatory of the University of Oxford from 1773 until 1934, and today forms part of Green Templeton College

The All Souls College towers by Nicholas Hawksmoor, architect of Westminster Abbey

This 1509 Magdelene Tower bell tower is part of Magdalen College

136   Oxford's elegant Hertford Bridge links two Hertford College buildings. Its popular name, the 'Bridge of Sighs', is due to the false belief it was a copy of the one in Venice

Merton College is one of the oldest in Oxford, with medieval buildings and a 13th century chapel as well as extensive gardens protected by the city wall

The Palladian-style Clarendon Building (front left), part of the Bodleian Libraries, sits alongside Sir Christopher Wren's D-shaped Sheldonian Theatre, built in the 1660s

Surrounding the Sheldonian Theatre are 13 square pillars topped with stone busts

These bearded, head-and-shoulder statues are known as the 'Sheldonian Emperors'

Although an iconic feature of Oxford's heritage, some mystery surrounds their purpose

The characterful Emperors have been a popular sight for 350 years

Folly Bridge in Oxford provides an ideal viewpoint to enjoy early morning mists as they rise above a smooth River Thames (traditionally known in Oxford as Isis)

Folly Bridge spans the River Thames via a central island that was originally a 900 AD oxen ford, and now features buildings including a crenellated Victorian tower

Collect them all ....

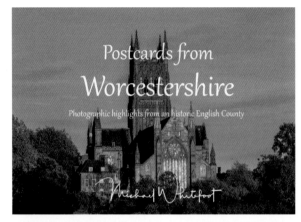

Postcards from
Worcestershire
Photographic highlights from an historic English County

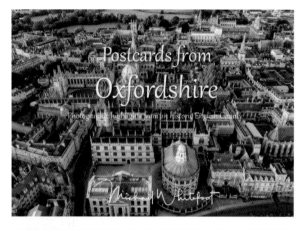

Postcards from
Oxfordshire
Photographic highlights from an historic English County

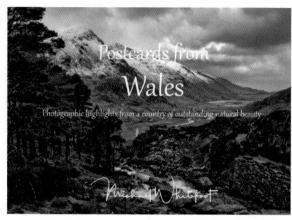

Postcards from
Wales
Photographic highlights from a country of outstanding natural beauty

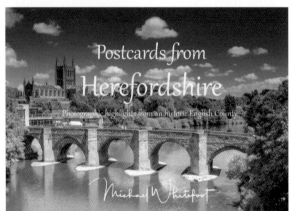

Postcards from
Herefordshire
Photographic highlights from an historic English County

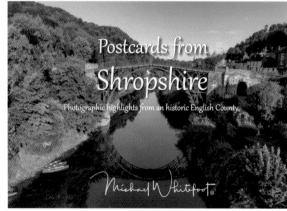

Postcards from
Shropshire
Photographic highlights from an historic English County

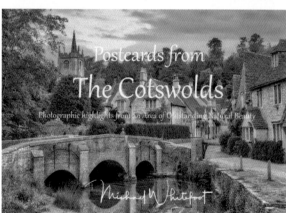

Postcards from
The Cotswolds
Photographic highlights from an Area of Outstanding Natural Beauty

www.michaelwhitefoot.co.uk